"I thought I had all the connections in my industry. Then I met Zachary Hall. His philosophy and approach to meeting new people and talking to strangers continues to pay dividends in my life and career. I've learned from Zach that even if you're sitting next to a soccer mom on a flight to Tulsa, give a conversation a chance. Everyone has a story that can potentially change your day or even your path in life."

Steven "Slippe" Lueder | DJ/Producer

* * *

"Zachary Hall is the consummate connector! No one escapes his power of prose, persuasion, and persistence! Sitting next to him on a plane would definitely be delightful, and it could lead to a real connection that could affect your future! An amazing "masked man," Zach is compassionate, energy abounding, and will not settle! He is a dear friend to me and my family—now and always! Don't Sleep on Planes is a super read!"

James S. Tonkin | Founder and President
Healthy Brand Builders

* * *

"I travel all over the world and am always shocked that no matter what city or country I'm in, I have people approach me daily to tell me that Zachary Hall is a mutual friend. It says a lot about the network of people in all walks of life that he has made an impact on. If you need anything in life, Zach knows a guy who will happily help. It's remarkable."

Frankie Muniz | Actor

"Every business owner needs a Zach Hall in their corner. Competition is stronger than ever, so it's crucial to create genuine and lasting relationships. Zach's network is large because he takes every opportunity to say hello to strangers and connect everyone he knows. A significant portion of our business is based on collaboration, and Zach has played a significant role in introducing us to influencers in our area."

Michael Spangenberg | Co-founder
State Forty Eight Clothing

* * *

"Zach and I met in college through laughter, no seriously. Since meeting at Phoenix College, he has changed my perspective on how to connect with people. As I travel the world playing soccer, I enjoy sharing laughter with fans of all ages. He's one of the few people I've met in my life that can motivate me to keep grinding and laugh on the way to success"

Jessica McDonald | Women's Professional Soccer Player
US National Team Member

* * *

"Zachary Hall is the greatest example of talk the talk AND walk the walk I've ever met. I've seen Zach live out every concept in this book, from meeting professional athletes to walking up to John McCain in a parking lot and holding his attention for a solid 15 minutes. This book will challenge your comfort zone, but if you go out and open yourself up to others you'll be shocked by how much they also open up to you. The connections and friendships you'll make by simply talking to people will change your life forever."

Kirk Newell | Sales Manager
Aruba

"It's interesting how some things work out in life. I was sitting in yet another mindless, sold-out Southwest flight to Las Vegas and before I could recruit an attractive woman for the middle seat beside me, Zachary Hall plopped himself down and began engaging me in random conversations. Looking back on that flight, and now in Zach's new book, I'm aware that his words of wisdom are very helpful in everyday human interactions."

Rollie V. Strum | Owner
Territory Incorporated

* * *

"Zach burst into my office, a whirlwind of energy behind a mascot's mask. As he laid waste to my desk, he purloined my business card and within a week we were having lunch and discussing his network and his future. I'm still not sure how it all happened, but we became fast friends. His approach to life is aggressive, savvy, and incredibly positive. What he's learned along the way is well worth reading and considering. His insights are enlightening and invigorating, and there's something here for everyone to take away and apply to their own life."

Dr. Bill Pepicello | Former President
University of Phoenix

* * *

"I felt like I knew Zach before I even met him in person. He continuously puts himself in positions to win, all with pure and genuine intentions. I've seen him network up close and personal, and you can absolutely trust him at his word. He might not look better than me (ever), but he's one of the best at connecting."

JD Whitfield | On-Air Radio Personality
CBS–103.3 AMP Radio Boston

DON'T
SLEEP ON
PLANES

DON'T SLEEP ON PLANES

Harness the Secret Power of Strangers to Increase Your Success and Fulfillment

Zachary Hall

JONES MEDIA PUBLISHING

Zachary Hall is available for speaking engagements. To make arrangements, please write to Zach@DontSleepOnPlanes.com

Jones Media Publishing
10645 N. Tatum Blvd. Ste. 200-166
Phoenix, AZ 85028
www.JonesMediaPublishing.com

Cover design and author photograph by Jennica E. Maes.

Printed in the United States of America

ISBN: 978-1-945849-15-2 paperback

To Meryl, the best connection
I ever made.

Contents

Introduction

*"It's time to start building your network
and letting the people you encounter
enrich your life while you enrich theirs."*

It was a Monday afternoon and I was scrambling to get out of the office to catch a 3:20 flight to Las Vegas on Southwest Airlines. I was excited to get out of Phoenix, take in the sights and sounds of the Strip, and join my peers for the first-ever professional mascot conference.

As I prepared to leave work, my to-do list felt like quicksand. I'd cross off one item and have to add two or three more. At the last possible moment, I climbed into an Uber and headed toward Sky Harbor Airport. Twenty minutes later, I found myself at the end of a long security line, hoping that I wouldn't miss my flight.

Once I got through security, I ran my tail off to get to my gate. With only seconds to spare, I was the last one on Flight 721. I heard the plane door close behind me as I greeted the flight attendant, who told me to find a seat quickly.

Immediately, I scanned my options. One of the benefits of flying Southwest (in addition to free bags and no change fees) is the ability to choose where you want to sit—or, more importantly for our purposes here, WHO you want to sit next to.

As always, I was hoping to find someone I could connect with, or at least enjoy sitting next to after such a hectic day. I didn't want to sit with anyone who was already engaged in their music, a movie, or a book. I had three choices: a middle-aged couple, a mom with a young child and a business-looking guy wearing a Rolex. I looked at his watch and thought that this guy had to be doing well at something, so I climbed over him and sat down in the center seat.

Mr. Businessman was definitely my best bet, especially since my own journey to Las Vegas was something of a business trip. The mascot conference was an idea that was long talked about among professional characters, a group I joined in 2009.

In fact, I helped get the event off the ground because of my extensive social network. Over the years, I've built solid relationships with just about anyone I could in Las Vegas, as this is a city where just about anything is possible with the right connections. I called all my contacts and arranged for free hotel rooms at the MGM Grand and Monte Carlo for my mascot compadres. I also arranged for meeting space, dinners, and shows each night— all provided free of charge from people in my network. These favors kept the conference budget extremely low, so it was easy for lots of other mascots to attend.

But I digress. At my moment of truth, on Southwest Flight 721, I had a single mission: Say hello to Mr. Businessman and engage in some good conversation about the career path he took to get a Rolex. I had about forty-five minutes of flying time and I wanted to make them count.

* * *

As it turned out, the conversation was so uplifting I wished we were flying to Australia.

After the basic etiquette of thanking my seatmates for letting me into their row, my opening comment to Mr. Businessman was a simple, "Vegas, huh?" I figured it would at least get me some information about why he was heading to Sin City.

He nodded politely but didn't say anything, and I realized I might have hit a snag trying to converse with him on this short flight. So naturally I asked a follow-up question, this time about his watch.

Boom! We made a connection.

I had just bought myself a watch as a reward for starting an MBA program. I told him about it, and went into a quick story I heard as a kid about the value of watches. "I've always believed that watches not only tell time, but also tell a moment in time," I said.

After the ice was broken, we exchanged some valuable information. He told me that he was affiliated with the Harvard Business School, and that he owned several large retail centers, two restaurants, a sports bar, and some nightclubs in the Vegas area.

I was attending the University of Phoenix, which I joked was the "Harvard of the Internet." That line got big laughs in one of my favorite movies, *The Internship*, and it got a chuckle from my newfound friend, Rollie Sturm. Rollie and I talked about business and life on that flight to Vegas in a very friendly, open way that would never have happened in a more formal interview session, and he told me to get in touch whenever I needed some friendly advice.

I've definitely kept in contact with Rollie over the years, and his encouragement after our chance meeting is one of the main reasons you're currently holding this book in your hands.

I really hope you can use the information in these pages to meet people like Rollie—and the many others who I'll introduce you to later—on your own. Whether you're on a plane, in a diner, or in the labyrinth of a big corporate office, deciding to say "Hi" to a stranger can make life much more interesting than zoning out with your music, reading a book, staring at your cell phone, or taking a nap.

While sharing simple moments with random people can spark mutually beneficial relationships, I want to make sure you understand that this book is NOT about trying to take advantage of people for personal gain. Networking has gotten a bad rap lately because people often focus less on giving and more on taking in their give-and-take relationships. This may be because people are jerks, but sometimes it's because people who might be on a lower rung of the success ladder don't think they have anything to offer people who appear to have "made it."

Trust me when I tell you that you have a lot more to offer, even to supposedly successful people, than you probably realize. Thanks to the trajectory of my career path, I've been able to hang out with an array of professional athletes, celebrities, business executives, and government officials over the years, and I know that many of these people value meaningful contact with everyday folks like you and me. In this book, I'll tell you how to make yourself more relevant and interesting to the people you meet along the way, and, I hope, give you the confidence you need to talk to people that may appear to be in another stratosphere.

* * *

So let's get to it. It's time to start building your network and letting the people you encounter enrich your life while you enrich theirs. It might not always be easy to get your courage up to start random conversations, but I really believe that it's one of the most important things you can do to have a successful life and career.

I'm a little worried that you might think it's easier for me to talk to people since my background as a mascot has put me in some very public situations. I'll admit that it IS a bit easier to do big and bold things when I have my costume on, but when it's just plain old me, I can be as shy and as intimidated as anyone else.

That's why I've come up with a unique approach to networking that can work for everyone. We'll talk about it in more detail later in the book, but the idea is that we can all find power, confidence, and purpose by embracing the masks—or M.A.S.K.s—we're always wearing every single day. Your M.A.S.K. is your mindset, attitude, sense, and knowledge—and I have a whole chapter devoted to showing you how you can use those aspects of your persona to open up to just about anybody.

I KNOW you can do this. I have faith that you can build a great network, and I'm going to teach you all my tricks and give you all my tips so you can meet people who will literally change your life. I really want you to put any fears and hesitations you may have aside, because you deserve to experience the power of connecting—or the power of NOT sleeping on planes.

Points Of Departure

- There are people around you every day—by choice and by accident. How you take advantage of these encounters can literally change your life.
- Be intentional about who you sit next to on an airplane. On my trip to Vegas, I wanted to sit next to a businessperson—not a bunch of fraternity guys.
- Everyone stresses out about travel, but it's cool to think you can make it more enjoyable by opening your mind up to, or at least sharing an experience with, someone you might not have otherwise met.

Flight Pattern

Choose to engage with someone on your next flight. If you're not going to be traveling soon, then find someone to sit next to at a lunch counter or bar and strike up a conversation. Networking is like dating—you need to put yourself out there.

Build Your Network

At the end of each chapter you're going to find a few contacts of mine that I'd like to share with you. You'll meet some of these people in the pages of this book, and you can get to know all of them a bit more at DontSleepOnPlanes.com. You'll also find a few blank spaces at the end of each chapter so you can list your own connections that come to mind as you're reading. I encourage you to work hard at building these relationships, and also to share your connections with the Don't Sleep on Planes (DSOP) community. Here are a few people I've met just by speaking up when our paths crossed. Feel free to reach out to them via their social handles, via Twitter or Instagram. They are leaders of industry, community, and influential contacts that I have been fortunate enough to connect with.

Name	Contact Info	Description
Jessica McDonald	@JMAC1422	Pro Soccer Player
Travis Hern	@TravisHearn	Impact Church Pastor
Julia Garcia	@JuliaGarciaNYC	Rewrite Project, Author, Speaker

1 The Art Of Talking To Strangers

"Whether you're with a stranger for forty-five minutes or four hours, you're always trying to forge the deepest bond you can....Every person you add to your network is really another way for you to help more people"

The standard advice we get at a very young age is that strangers are dangerous. This may be good counsel when we're five or ten, or even eighteen, but when we become adults the same rules don't necessarily apply.

Of course we need to be cautious as we go through the world, but it's important to keep things in perspective. If you really think about it, we meet and interact with strangers all the time:

- We need strangers to take risks on us when we're applying for jobs
- We hope a stranger on LinkedIn will accept our request to learn more about his or her company
- Strangers cook for us and serve food to us whenever we go to a new restaurant
- Friendly strangers are everywhere!

Effective networking is just selecting the right strangers. Our society is able to function because, for the most part, people are trustworthy. There'll always be a few bad apples, but with a little awareness and common sense, most of us get through life relatively unscathed. The occasional jerk we encounter usually isn't enough to deter us from continuing to forge new relationships.

* * *

The closest people in my life started out as strangers, and almost every day I'm amazed at how quickly a new person can jump from the status of stranger to friend simply through a shared experience, a common interest, or a referral from someone we both know.

I was recently in New York City enjoying a quick meal at an Italian restaurant in Chelsea. Naturally, I was eating solo at the bar, waiting to find someone to talk to. A nice couple sat next to me and we began chatting. We ended up connecting over wine—they bottle their own at home—and Billy Joel, who was playing that night at Madison Square Garden. We were both going to the show and, as it turned out, had tickets just three rows apart from each other!

When we said our good-byes, I gave them my business card (I hand out a LOT of business cards and I suggest you do the same!) and told them to look me up if they ever came to Phoenix, especially if they wanted to see a baseball game. I didn't think much about it afterward, but when I got home a couple of days later and went back to work, a few bottles of home-bottled wine were waiting for me on my desk!

When you cross paths with someone at a restaurant, on a plane, or anywhere else, your lives are temporarily intertwined. That's why it just makes sense to open yourself up to building a connection. You don't have to always be like Buddy the Elf (more on this later), but you have a lot to gain by having friendly conversations with people you don't know.

Take Advantage Of Your Captive Audience

Every chance you get to talk to someone new is a golden opportunity to grow your personal or professional network. What's great about a plane flight is that you have a captive audience who's literally invading your personal space for usually an hour or more.

Think about what it's like when you get together with a close friend, or even a family member. Most of the time they're at least four feet away from you. But on a plane, I'm in your bubble—the least you can do is say "Hi!"

In addition to the awkward proximity, you also have a lot of built-in things to talk about when you sit next to someone on an airplane:

- You're both going to the same destination
- You're both glad you aren't sitting next to that crying baby
- You're both praying for a nice landing
- You're both anxious to get moving

The person next to you is a sitting duck for a great conversation because you've already got so much in common! I truly am amazed that so many people retreat into their music, their videos, their work or their books on a flight when they could make a great connection instead. I realize that not every person you sit next to or come across in life will be interested in spending time connecting, but why not take a shot?

The key is to find common ground as quickly as possible. The fact that you're both on the same flight is a good starting point, but you have to dig deeper if you want a real connection. Do you share a love for the same city? Do you both like the same sports team, band, TV show, or movie? Is there any overlap in your work? Common hobbies? A similar style or fashion sense?

Look for clues to make the deepest connections possible. Clothing can be a huge giveaway—for example, I love seeing people with baseball hats on! Without invading someone's privacy, you should always do a quick scan for things like logos, accents, objects (musical instruments, for example), and fragrances in a search for common ground.

I sat between two guys on a flight once, and because I took the time to talk to each one of them separately, I discovered that they were both in the same business. Before long, I introduced them to each other right on the plane and helped both of them make a valuable connection.

If you don't try to talk to a seatmate, you might miss out on something really amazing or cool about the person sitting THAT CLOSE to you:

- They might run a company you've dreamed of working for
- They might live in a part of the country you want to move to
- They might have a life lesson they can teach you
- They could either become—or introduce you to—your future spouse

The options and outcomes are endless, but it all hinges on that initial spark that feeds the flame of connection. Just say "Hi" and see where it takes you!

Don't Lead With "How Are You?"

Think about what happens when you ask someone how they're doing, especially if it's someone you don't know really well. You might get a "good" or "fine" in response—and that'll be that. People will usually meet their obligation to answer your question, but they won't often give you much else to go on.

Quite frankly, short, dead-end conversations won't help you build the network you're looking to grow. So you have to come up with a strategy to make a deeper connection as quickly as possible.

I read a fascinating post on Quora recently by a guy named Dan Chang, founder of thefriendformula.com. In this short post, he outlines the types of questions you need to ask to deepen a conversation.

Dan explains that people go through the following progression as they share information and build a connection:

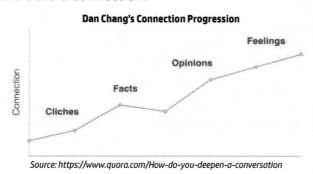

Dan Chang's Connection Progression

Source: https://www.quora.com/How-do-you-deepen-a-conversation

He asserts that most people miss out on deeper connections because they get stuck in the comfort zone of clichés and facts. It's easy to talk about the weather, for example, and you can do it with anyone—no real connection necessary.

If you want to take things to the next level, Dan recommends moving from "WHAT to WHY" as quickly as possible. Doing this requires the ability to ask specific questions that get specific answers involving the other person's opinions and feelings.

I totally agree with what Dan has to say, and I've naturally built the same kind of process into my own approach to networking. It takes some practice, but even subtle things like asking "How's your day going so far?" instead of "How are you?" will lead to more interesting dialog. Here are some more examples of questions that I use to help open people up and get them talking about their opinions and feelings:

- **Vegas, huh?**

This is my go-to question on a plane, and I'll use whatever city we're both flying to. Not only does it establish common ground right away, it opens up a possible conversation in just a couple of words.

And it works nine times out of ten—Rollie Strum was the exception that proves the rule.

- **How about that game last night?**

If the person sitting next to you is sporting a team logo and you know that team had a big win or loss the night before, this can be a GREAT question to ask.

- **What are some good restaurants in Chicago?**

Chicago is just an example—use the name of the city they're from or the one you're both going to.

- **What's it like to be a professional watercolorist?**

Use whatever job or occupation the other person discloses. If you have friends or family members who do the same thing, be sure to share a story or two from your own experience.

Mix it up and try different things to see what works for you. Just remember that meeting strangers is like a first date, so you need to be careful what you say and how you say it. Not everyone is willing to open up easily. So, as with any first conversation, it's usually a safe bet to avoid taboo subjects like politics and religion.

No matter where you are—on a plane, at a restaurant, etc.—it's great to start a conversation with WHERE YOU BOTH ARE:

- "Can you believe that crying baby?"
- "I hope it's not raining in Seattle when we land!"
- "Have you had the grilled cheese here?"
- "This place has the best clam chowder."

After you've established the fact that you're sharing the same space and time with someone, you can branch out from there. If you love TV, talk about that. Are you funny? Tell a joke or a story that relates to your current situation with this other person. Or, if you see that someone's eating a food you like, start an expansive conversation about that: "You ordered shrimp? Have you ever been to Maryland? They have the best!"

You get the idea—look for unique ways to start conversations and you'll be way ahead of the game when it comes to making connections. Just remember, this all comes back to YOU and your willingness to open up and be mindful about getting beyond "good."

Start Every Relationship On "Probe-ation"!

Even unique introduction questions don't always work their magic. As I said earlier, not everyone is willing to get outside their comfort zone and discuss opinions and feelings with a stranger.

While you ultimately have to respect that, it never hurts to try a little gentle probing to turn things around. The key is to avoid coming on too strong, and knowing when to back down.

I've found that it's pretty easy to get someone's name, find out what they do for a living, learn what they like to do for fun, discover if they have any kids or not, etc. Getting that type of factual information is valuable, and because it's non-threatening, can help relax the other person.

Here's a typical interaction that could have stopped at any time without some consistent probing:

Zach: Chicago, huh?!

Fellow Passenger: (*Smiles politely and goes back to her book.*)

Zach: Are you going for work or fun?

Fellow Passenger: Work.

Zach: Oh, cool. What do you do?

Fellow Passenger: I work in sales.

Zach: Oh yeah? What kind of sales?

Fellow Passenger: I sell glassware to bars and restaurants.

Zach: Wow. You must have some fun stories. I'm open to trying a new bar when I get to Chicago. Can you tell me your favorites?

Fellow Passenger: Sure. Do you like beer or cocktails?

At this point we've opened up a new line of conversation that's based on what my seatmate thinks about different bars and drinks. She's sharing her opinions and feelings with me in less than thirty seconds!

I'm learning something about what she's passionate about, filing it away for future reference, and thinking of stories to tell her that she might enjoy or find useful in some way. Before we know it, the plane is landing, we're both feeling energized, and we've shared our contact information and a promise to stay in touch.

With a little probing, you can steer a superficial interaction to the point where the other person is fully engaged and even asking YOU questions! And when you've both opened up, you've dramatically increased the possibility of a long-lasting connection.

Don't be afraid of probing, and don't be afraid of rejection. Nine times out of ten you might be put off by people but if you're persistent, that tenth person could change your life in amazing ways. Consider this fact about professional ball players: Those who go three for ten are considered legendary. The greatest players FAIL seventy percent of the time! It's the same with networking. Not everyone you meet is going to be the missing link that connects all the dots of your life, but if you keep going up to bat and practicing your skills, you might be pleasantly surprised at how much richer your life becomes. We'll see YOU in the networking hall of fame!

Bridging The Generation Gap

My fellow millennials need help probing upward, and I've found that older people need help probing downward as both generations faced different upbringings. I love meeting people of all ages, so I try to connect with people from different generations whenever I can. I know this practice is helpful to me, even if I screw things up.

One thing I've learned is that sometimes what I'm wearing makes it harder for an older person to take me seriously. But since I like to be comfortable on a plane, I work on changing my language, not my wardrobe, to be more relatable to people outside my age range. At the same time, if I'm going to a nice event and dress the part, I find it much easier to "network up" with older attendees.

Just because someone is young and inexperienced doesn't mean they can't help someone who's older and more successful. As a young person, you might not be able to offer wisdom, but you can offer enthusiasm, energy, a fresh perspective on a topic, and even knowledge about what's cool or current. Never sell yourself, or your personal life story, short!

Inside Jokes Can Lead To Serious Connections

Once you establish as much common ground as you can with a new contact, the next step is to deepen the relationship in the moment. What stories and inside jokes can you develop with each other while you're on a plane or in a restaurant? How can you create a lasting bond?

I met a woman on a plane once who paints watercolor paintings. It's really incredible! This woman gets paid to travel to cool places like Catalina, Coronado, Cape Cod, and Capri—and those are just the C's! She gets to take people to the forest or the beach and paint. Talking to her made me think about how great it would be to get people to join me in exotic places and make that my living.

Now, I never would have talked to this woman and gotten her perspective on life and work if I didn't sit next to her on a plane and strike up a conversation. She was planning on reading, but I broke the ice by making her my accomplice in a potential felony I was committing!

A few hours before Doris and I met on the plane, I was hanging out in an airport bar, trying to strike up a conversation with two businessmen who were on my same short flight from San Diego to Phoenix. They weren't that talkative, and kind of gave me the brush-off because I was wearing shorts and a sports jersey, so I finally gave up and did some work on my computer.

When I was packing up to catch my flight, I noticed that one of the guys had left his laptop at the bar. I took it with me, expecting to see the guy again at the gate and give it back to him.

I didn't see the guy in the waiting area, but I knew he had to be on that plane. I was in the C group on this flight and I figured I'd run into him while I was looking for a seat, but I didn't see him. When I did sit down next to the watercolor lady, I told her the whole story. I had this lost laptop with me and I didn't know what to do.

So my new friend Doris and I had a great time talking about all the trouble we could get into just for doing something nice for someone. We created lots of inside jokes on that flight, and now I have a watercolor lady for life if I ever need one.

As we landed and exited the plane, I was quick to look for this guy in the terminal area. I found him yelling at his coworker about leaving the laptop behind. As I approached him, you should have seen his face. I saved his life!

We're going to talk about what I call good bricks and bad bricks later, but let me tell you, this guy was a bad brick. I'll reveal his response to me in chapter 5. If you want to skip ahead, it's on page 83.

Stay In The Moment For The Most Long-Term Gain

Whether you're with a stranger for forty-five minutes or four hours, you're always trying to forge the deepest bond you can.

During that initial interaction you might get a funny story, some good advice, or just a different perspective on something you've been thinking about or maybe even struggling with. The point is to enjoy the moment without thinking too much about any possible future benefits of the relationship.

If you're going to think long-term, you should really be thinking about how you could help the other person, or how they could interact with other people in your network.

In my view, the real point of networking is to help you live a more service-based life. Every person you add to your network is really another way for you to help more people. The best thing about having an expansive network is the ability to connect someone who has a service with someone else who needs it.

Now, you might be thinking, "What's in it for me?"

Well, if you really need to know, I'll tell you: With a solid network, YOU suddenly become the person with all the power. You're the connector. The deal maker. The mover and shaker! You get to make all kinds of great things happen for all the great people in your life. And trust me—if you live your life that way, you'll get a lot more back than you ever thought possible.

Points Of Departure

- The people you meet may be able to help you, but think about how you can help them, and also about how they might be able to help other people in your network.

Adopt a giving mindset over a taking mindset and everything will find its way.

- If you find yourself traveling or eating alone, it's easier to open up to strangers, aka your captive audience. Give it a shot!

- If you take a chance and engage someone in conversation, they may change your life. If you bury yourself in your phone or social media, focusing on what other people are doing outside your immediate area, you could miss out on an exciting opportunity with someone right in front of you.

- Bring your A game when you meet someone. You've only got one chance to make a first impression.

- Use clues—like team or band logos and computer or clothing brands—to turn someone from stranger to friend more quickly. Sharing interests and experiences can go a long way toward creating a lasting relationship.

- Gentle probing, using specific and progressively more meaningful questions, can open people up to the possibility of a great conversation and a real connection.

Flight Patterns

1. Look at all the strangers around you. This week introduce yourself to a handful of people you've never met. To increase your chances of making valuable connections, go to places where you'll find people with similar interests, or people who'll inspire you in some way. If I want coffee, for example, I'll often go to a place I know where successful professionals and entrepreneurs are always crushing emails and working on proposals.

2. Start greeting your friends and family members with the intention to go further than "How are you?" Try asking follow-up questions that require something more than a yes or no answer.

Build Your Network

Has a stranger you sought out become a valued contact? Write down the names, contact info (phone, email, twitter, etc.), and a short description of anyone you think of from reading this chapter. I'll get you started with some people I've struck up random conversations with:

Name	Contact Info	Description
Doris Rice	www.DorisRice.com	Watercolor painter
James Wennlund	@JamesWennlundRJ	V.P., Raymond James
Jim Tonkin	@HealthyBrandBuilders	President, Healthy Brand Builders (Instagram)

2 A World Of Connections

"If you don't have the success you want right now, you can make some real headway by starting to become more significant to more people."

Now that you know how easy it can be to go from stranger to valued connection, it's time to add people to your network on a regular basis. Airplanes are great, but even if you're not a jet-setter you have lots of opportunities to meet new people every single day.

I try to make new connections all the time, not just when I'm traveling. I don't wake up every day saying to myself, "I've got to make new connections today," but I do go through each day with an open mind and an open heart toward anyone whose path crosses mine. I might just say a passing hello to someone on the street. I might go out of my way to show appreciation to someone who gives me great service at a restaurant. And I'll always seize opportunities to meet people at a bar or restaurant counter.

Growing my network and hearing people's stories gets me jazzed up, so I try to do it every chance I get. And for me that usually means taking time out of each day to put away the smartphone and tune into the incredible human beings all around me. Don't get me wrong, I'm a HUGE social media fan and I maintain my network using the latest tech tools, but the best connections are generally the ones that happen in person.

I really believe that we need quality flesh-and-blood time with peers, mentors, friends, etc., to achieve our dreams and reach our goals—or to at least make life more fun.

Here's a story that really ticks me off. In high school I was fortunate to have served as class president my senior year, and it was my responsibility a decade later to plan my class's ten-year reunion. This glorious event occurred in 2015, so I created a Westview High School Class of 2005 Facebook group, got out my old yearbooks, and sent friend requests to all my classmates.

Social media made it easy to contact everyone, and I wanted them all to come to the reunion. But I quickly came to believe that Facebook was ruining our event. So many of us already knew what everyone else was up to—even what they had for dinner the night before—that a lot of people skipped the actual physical reunion.

About 100 people from our 600+ class came together for a night of fun, good cheer, and laughter. We had a great time, but the people who didn't come missed out on the joy of being in the same room with everyone else. I really felt sorry for them!

My point is this: If you have an email-only, text-only, Facebook-only, or even phone-only paradigm with someone, break it once in a while and meet for lunch or a cup of coffee. It'll change your perspective, and will definitely deepen your connections.

You Gotta Eat, You Gotta Network!

Have you ever wished you could get more time with someone at work you're trying to grow with? Or that you could get to know that contact you made at a happy hour a few weeks ago?

To that, I say—MEALS!

Meals are built-in networking opportunities and we all have three of them every single day— four or five if you count coffee breaks! I don't care if you're on a budget or on a diet, at some point you need to consume food. And what better way to find common ground with someone than to share a meal with them!

While it may not always be economical, I try to find someone to eat lunch with or have coffee with each day. I've worked in organizations with more than 150 people, so I could literally have lunch with a different person every day for several months if I could schedule it!

If I'm by myself, I'll go to a restaurant with a counter or a bar and let the adventure flow. I don't always end up meeting someone, but I'm always ready for it to happen. Chance meal encounters are especially valuable, and I don't want to let one slip away by eating at my desk alone! How many meals are you letting go to waste if your true intention is to develop or strengthen your network?

The Brick House Perspective On Networking

As we grow up, we're encouraged to make friends, set goals, and continue our personal development. As a kid, it began to dawn on me that I should start thinking of the people in my life as "bricks" I could use to build a better "house," or future, for myself.

This idea has become a lasting metaphor for how much support I get from people I encounter along my life's journey. Some people are beautiful bright red bricks that add value to my house. Other people are dull, crumbly bricks. These are people who took more than they gave, or just tried to knock me down because they were nervous, pessimistic, jealous, or whatever. These bricks don't provide ongoing support, and although they'll always be part of my history—my house—they hold less and less significance as time goes by.

Every day I'm drawing the blueprints to the home I'm trying to build, and because I'm always growing my network, my house keeps getting bigger and more beautiful. I have entire rooms with bricks that represent teachers, friends, colleagues, mentors, relatives, and other people I've met at critical times in my life.

I'm always looking for bright red bricks to add to my house, and you should, too. But where do you find them? The choices you make—where you go to school, what career you decide on, even where you go to lunch—all help determine what kind of bricks you're going to meet.

While actual connections are random, you can put yourself in a better position for meeting more influential people, just like I did when I met Jim Tonkin at a charity dinner. He's a beverage guru and part of the team that brought Arnold Palmer—

the guy—to Arizona Iced Tea so they could bottle Arnold Palmer—the drink. Our chance interaction, which deepened over a shared passion for baseball, has given me an awesome mentor.

You can also seek out bricks for your house by approaching specific people you want to meet. Even if it's a long shot, most people will accept an invitation to coffee. If they don't, it's a small sign that the relationship might take some extra work, or maybe that you've stumbled upon a dull brick that you don't want as part of your house anyway.

It's been important for me to seek out some strong red bricks because I kept running into dull bricks as a kid growing up in west Phoenix. In addition to typical peer pressure, my parents went through a divorce when I was young and I had to learn to bounce between two neighborhoods and deal with different friends in each one. The one bright spot was the Rollero Family Skating Center where I could enjoy a good time without the fear of gangs or drugs.

My first red brick outside my family was the guy who owned this place, Tom Wyse. When I was just ten years old, I offered to help clean his family business during the week if he'd let me skate for free on the weekends so I could hang out with my friends.

Because I loved his business and took pride in my work, Mr. Wyse and his wife took me under their wing and mentored me. They gave me meals and taught me about business, especially the value of time and hard work, while I did things like take out the trash and clean the bathrooms.

Tom even taught me about the importance of networking. One day when I was about thirteen years old, he took me aside and said, "You know, son, there are two types of people in this world— spark plugs and butt plugs. One stinks and the other one drives the world. So which one do you want to be?" While it probably wasn't the most appropriate thing for a grownup to say to a thirteen-year-old, I knew at that point that I wanted to drive the world!

I worked for the Wyse's for six years as I went from wanting to skate for free to saving money for my first car. They helped me grow as a leader, and as a young man, in immeasurable ways. Meeting them made me realize how much help you can get from someone if you offer to help them first.

Another Perspective: Tend To Your "Garden"

If the house analogy doesn't quite do it for you, another approach I like is to think of your network as a garden. I was fortunate to have had a life coach for six months when I was in a collegiate leadership program and she taught me this perspective on networking.

Basically, all your connections are plants that you need to tend to.

Some people are flowers. Others are vegetables. And still others are weeds. Every day you use your energy—your bucket of water and your weed whacker—to help all the flowers and vegetables thrive.

How you use your energy is a never-ending balancing act. Some days you might overwater certain plants. Other days you might forget a particular flower bed or inadvertently ignore the tomatoes. And some days you're so worn out from distributing your water that you procrastinate when it comes to killing the weeds.

The garden approach has helped me get over my constant struggles with FOMO—the fear of missing out. My natural instinct to say "yes" to everything fun has wreaked havoc on some of the most important plants in my garden and impacted my work/life balance.

Now that I'm in my thirties, I make sure that I devote some of my water to nurturing the personal and professional relationships I really want to maintain for decades to come.

If you work your entire life to make connections, build your network, and increase your net worth but begin to neglect important things like your family, your significant other (SO) your health, etc., then you really haven't built much after all.

As your network grows, be prepared to spend more time maintaining your most important relationships to keep them growing.

The Commercial That
Led To A Free MBA

After a few years of working as a performer with professional sports teams in Arizona, I realized that I kept putting off my entrepreneurial ambitions. So I decided to go back to school and earn my MBA.

Shortly after making that decision, I was assigned to do a TV spot for the University of Phoenix. The largest private online school in the United States had recently signed on as a huge team sponsor and we shot this ridiculously hilarious commercial to promote the new partnership.

The scenario was that my character was president of the school for a day. So we took over the real president's office and just trashed it for comic effect. The commercial went viral, but I felt bad for the school president who had to put everything back in its place.

Naturally, I saw this as an opportunity to connect with him. I grabbed one of his business cards from his desk on my way out, and when I got back to the stadium, I invited him to lunch via email.

Two weeks later we had a great meeting. I mentioned that I was thinking of going to Grad school, and he told me that the university had some great scholarships and financing options through the new partnership with the team. I applied for a full-ride university scholarship, explained my passion for business, and used my network to generate some great recommendations. Two years later, I earned my MBA—free of charge.

I didn't beg this guy for a favor. I simply did the right thing by inviting him to lunch. I was able to take advantage of my captive audience, found some common ground, and asked him to join me for an activity we both had to do anyway—eat.

He quickly saw how serious I was about advancing my education. And because he believes in a service-lead life just like I do, he gave me valuable information that I was able to put to good use.

Success Vs. Significance

I believe we all want to be successful in life, but wouldn't you rather be significant in someone else's life? Fortunately, the two often go hand in hand. Greater success can magnify the significance of your life, and greater significance can lead to greater success.

Can you see the beauty in this? If you don't have the success you want right now, you can make some real headway by starting to become more significant to more people.

Instead of complaining about your job, for example, reach out to people outside your company and see how you can help them in ways that you're really passionate about. This will help you focus on the things that really matter to you, and may even lead you on a new career path.

It took five people helping me to get my foot in the door in the sports industry. And every year since, about five more people have helped me grow in my field. That's how the world works, and today I constantly think about how I can be one of those people to others in their efforts to grow.

Believe it or not, not all of the people who helped me were directly tied to the sports industry. Getting to know my pastor, for example, helped me have conversations with people in my realm that I never would have been able to have before. These conversations have led to important connections with world-class athletes and business leaders through the common bond of a shared faith.

I like meeting and being open to all kinds of people, because you never know when or where the information you get from them will be useful. It's like my watercolor lady—I can't wait for the day I can connect someone with her, or better yet find time to go on one of her excursions.

The Power Of The Unexpected

The idea of serendipity is exciting, especially when you're single. You never know when, where, or how the person who's missing in your life is going to show up. When I met my significant other, I was volunteering for a local charity's hunger campaign, which she was running as the organization's marketing lead.

Growing up I dealt with various forms of food insecurities, and at times I depended on food boxes from different nonprofit organizations. To this day my favorite foods are pretty basic—pasta, cereal, and other simple staples that come in a package or can. As I've grown as a leader within my community, I've committed to sharing my story to help where I can, and this particular charity event was a natural opportunity. However, I had no idea how my commitment to this event would change my life for the better.

I could have easily kept quiet, but I really wanted to make a difference, and I think that honest, personal testimony is incredibly powerful. So I opened up to this young lady about what happened to me as a kid. This had the unexpected side benefit of making a deep connection between us, and today we look forward to spending the rest of our lives together!

I haven't lived a charmed life by any stretch of the imagination, but I'm creating one each time I make a connection with the people who cross my path. Trust me, there IS a world of connections out there that can change your life. No matter the status of the people around you, the people you look up to, or the people waiting in line with you, each individual forging a path forward has experienced joys and hardships in their past.

Knowing that should make it easier to talk to anyone!

Speaking Of The Power Of The Unexpected "..."

Shortly after I began my relationship with my significant other, I was working with a contact on an event at Top Golf, a driving range/entertainment venue in Gilbert, Arizona. This event allowed high-end donors to hang out and hit golf balls with professional athletes, and the money raised went to a variety of local charities.

Through my network, I invited a few athletes to support the event, including quarterback John Skelton and baseball players Archie Bradley, David Hernandez, Patrick Corbin, and Kaleb Fleck. My actor friend Frankie Muniz also agreed to help out.

As I walked from bay to bay at the driving range, placing athletes with donors, I fortuitously put Archie Bradley with Dave and Mary Staley and Jason and Sandi Job. By the end of the event, these amazing people were having such a great time that they offered Archie and me the opportunity to join them at the football all-star game the following day.

Knowing that my significant other wasn't into football, I ended up taking my friend Tyler Vasquez along for the ride. He was the biggest football fan I knew, and he also managed the Boys & Girls Club for which I was a board member. We all met up at the Staley residence, and when a big limo pulled up, I knew it was going to be a special day.

During our ride to the game, we continued to get to know each other. Tyler and I talked about how we became friends as kids, and why we were so committed to the Boys & Girls Clubs. We mentioned that our chapter was in the middle of a major campaign to raise funds to build a football field on some vacant land nearby. It was just a natural conversation and we really didn't think much of it, but at the end of the day, Jason and Dave gave us more than $20,000 to make this field a reality!

This one random connection led to an incredible legacy, which will have a lasting impact on thousands of kids for many years to come, in addition to some amazing new friends with whom I continue to enjoy traveling, dining out, and going to sporting events.

Calculated Risks Can Bring Big Rewards

Here's another example of how an ordinary day can turn into an extraordinary one because of a random, unexpected connection. I was meeting a childhood friend who recently quit her job to start her own wedding planning and events company after successfully planning her own amazing wedding.

Liz and I both grew up in the same low-income neighborhood and worked at the same roller rink for Tom and Beth Wyse. While I went the academic route by going to college after high school, Liz went straight into the corporate world and climbed the ladder at Bank of America. After making it all the way to the VP level, she decided to give it all up and start her own business. She is a force of nature!

I was excited to meet with her and pick her brain, and we also planned to discuss how some of my connections could help her new business succeed. Oh, and she naturally tried to get me to propose to my aforementioned significant other because she wanted to plan MY wedding.

We met at a local hot spot in the Biltmore area of Phoenix and were told that we'd have to wait a long time if we wanted a table. Instead, we went to one of my favorite places in any restaurant—the counter.

A few minutes after we sat down, a familiar face sat next to my friend. It was Scott Flansburg, aka the Human Calculator. I had met him briefly a few times before, but a number of my connections knew him really well.

As he sat down, I said hello and followed up with, "You're the Human Calculator guy, right?" He said yes, and I quickly let him know how we knew each other. The entire shape of my meeting with Liz quickly changed with Scott engaged. The three of us talked about life, the power of the number 9, and the many places around the world that his love of numbers has taken him.

This chance encounter helped bring him into my circle (and my friend's), and allowed me to seek his advice on writing the book YOU are enjoying today. As a best-selling author, he had a lot of great insights for me!

The World Of Connections Keeps Growing

We're more mobile than ever these days, which makes it easier to meet people from all over the world. By extension, that means you'll be more likely to help people in more places with a far-flung network.

There's certainly no shortage of people to meet. In the United States alone, 318.9 million of us are spread across the fifty states. There are 285 American cities with populations of more than 100,000. And there are more than 5,000 public airports according to the U.S. Department of Transportation.

So what are you going to do tomorrow? I'd say the odds are in your favor to build a new connection, and here's just another story to illustrate how randomly awesome it can be.

Earlier I mentioned going to a charity event with Frankie Muniz, the actor. The way we first connected was pretty random, and it's a funny story.

I'm sure you remember the TV show *Malcolm in the Middle*. All through high school my buddies used to tease me by saying that I looked just like the main character. Fast forward to 2010 when I got an invitation from someone in my network to attend the Muhammad Ali Fight Night XV in Phoenix. I was excited for the opportunity to meet Muhammad Ali and all the other cool guests who were expected to attend, but I had no idea that I was going to connect with my doppelgänger!

So I get to the event all dressed up in a gray suit with a blue shirt and a red tie—the friend who invited me forgot to mention that it was a black-tie affair! I was cool with it, and so was everyone at the event, but I still laugh about it to this day.

Despite my wardrobe challenges, I met tons of great people at this event, and I have a great photo of me in my gray suit and Frankie in his designer tux. I thought we really hit it off so I gave him my business card (that's just what I do) so we could keep in touch. I never heard from the guy, probably because I was dressed like a clown at a formal party, but if nothing else, I'm a pretty patient person.

About a year and a half later, I ran into Frankie at a Suns game. I was hanging out with a few of my athlete buddies who were promoting a celebrity basketball game the following day. When we saw Frankie, my friends introduced themselves and we all ended up talking for a while. As we connected again, we realized that we had more than our looks in common, so I invited him to hang out with my group any time he wanted. He's not the most social guy in the world, but over the past six years we've become best friends!

In the end, sometimes you have to wait it out for random encounters to turn into meaningful contacts. Some of the advertising guys I know talk about the concept of reach and frequency. In a nutshell, it means that you have to hit your target audience repeatedly with the right messaging to eventually persuade them to buy your product or service. If you're lucky (or strategic) enough to run into the same people over and over again, you'll have a better chance of adding them to your personal networking universe.

Points Of Departure

- Why sit at a table by yourself when you can sit at the counter or bar and meet someone like the Human Calculator?
- Someone you meet today could change your life instantaneously. Be genuine with everyone you encounter, and try to figure out how YOU can help THEM.
- The more significance you can bring to other people, the more success you'll achieve.

Flight Pattern

Think about what your brick house or your garden looks like—and how you want it to look. Describe it in writing. Draw a picture of it. Decide how to collect more red bricks, or figure out better ways to distribute your water. Don't limit yourself, and work hard to make the connections you need to build the house or grow the garden of your dreams!

Build Your Network

Think about the worlds you live in (career, hobbies, volunteer activities, sports, etc.) and the places you frequent. Write down the names, contact info (phone, email, twitter, etc.), and a short description of the people you've already met on your life's journey. I'll get you started with some people I've crossed paths with:

Name	Contact Info	Description
Scott Flansburg	@HumanCalculator	The Human Calculator
Liz Marcou	@25EventManagement	Wedding/event planner
Frankie Muniz	@FrankieMuniz	Actor, musician

3 Embrace Your M.A.S.K.

*"When you have your M.A.S.K. on,
it protects you so you can be more
outgoing, take more risks, and definitely
change your approach to things to get the
results you're looking for."*

Do you ever think about HOW you're going to get certain things done? Like if you have a long day at work—how are you going to have enough energy to do all the things you have to do at home? Or if you have a late night out, how are you going to prepare for the next day's sales calls or meetings?

My answer to this is to always wear the right M.A.S.K. at the right time. With the right MINDSET,

ATTITUDE, SENSE, and KNOWLEDGE, you'll get the superpowers you need to get things done.

Think of Halloween or themed dances back in high school. You would dress up as a pirate or a monster or a famous person, and then play the part without even thinking about it. When you have your M.A.S.K. on, it protects you so you can be more outgoing, take more risks, and definitely change your approach to things to get the results you're looking for.

In A M.A.S.K. You Can Do Just About Anything

Working as a professional mascot has given me many highs. After all, guys like me in costume get to do lots of outrageous stunts. While embracing the mask of my character, I've rappelled down buildings, entertained kids with country music superstar Garth Brooks, performed on Broadway with the cast of *Cats*, and, of course, I've appeared at stadiums all over the world, danced like a fool on national TV, and much more.

I couldn't do any of it as Zachary Hall, but my mask gives me superpowers. And your mask can do the same for you. Whatever your service is, it can become the M.A.S.K. that helps you deliver your very best in every situation, whether you're looking for a job, acquiring more customers, or searching for new opportunities to explore.

We wear multiple masks every day—as friends, parents, siblings, employees, employers, etc. If you embrace the masks that YOU wear and let them guide you, you really can do amazing things outside your comfort zone. Here's how it works:

Mindset

This is where you put your own troubles, cares, and fears aside so you can stay focused on your task at hand. Because your mindset comes from your inner feeling about what you want to achieve and accomplish, it's largely supported by the level of interest, enthusiasm, and passion that you bring to the table.

Attitude

Attitude is your approach to each situation after you've gotten into the proper mindset, and is influenced by your beliefs and values, your level of confidence, and your concern for yourself and others. When I'm in my mascot costume, my attitude is that I have to be a catalyst for happiness and joy.

Sense

This is your ability to read the room and decide in each moment what you need to do to go with the flow. In addition to your immediate feeling in a given situation, you can draw on research and historical evidence to get a better sense of things.

Knowledge

As you go through life, you increase the amount of evidence and information you can use to inform your sense of any situation. The larger the body of knowledge you have, the better able you'll be to keep momentum going and pivot, if necessary.

If you can absorb these concepts, then you can keep meeting amazing people all the time like I do. I can honestly say that there's NOTHING special about me, other than the fact that I approach random encounters with intention and invest in networking as a life-enhancing activity. I'm just like everyone else, but I've learned to apply a few simple techniques that set me up to meet great people and turn random personal interactions into real connections. These are the same techniques you can learn from this playbook.

I understand that building a social network through purposeful contact with strangers isn't going to be easy for everyone. I don't always feel like going out on a limb to approach people, but I do it anyway because I know that if I really embrace my M.A.S.K., ANY interaction can impact the direction of my hopes and dreams.

I've shared a few moments when I've made some incredible contacts, and other moments when my approach didn't work out so well. At the end of the day, I never take any of it personally because everyone is different, and sometimes the timing just isn't right. I don't wake up every day with a tote board of networking goals, but I do leave the house wearing my M.A.S.K.

* * *

I've found that I'm much better interacting with people when I embrace my M.A.S.K. I developed this technique while working as a professional mascot, but when I got to thinking about it, I realized that we're all mascots to a certain degree.

Professional mascots wear a literal mask. And each time I've put one on I knew that I had to embrace the character that people expected to see. There are mascots everywhere: theme parks, sporting events, mall stores, fast food restaurants. Each of these characters comes to life because of an individual who's tasked with embracing that mask.

I got to thinking about what it took to consistently embrace the essence of my character, and I came up with this simple acronym—M.A.S.K.

When I'm behind the literal mask of my mascot costume, I'm representing a brand that will outlast me. Kids remember their time with my character, but they don't have a clue who Zachary Hall is. That's as it should be, so when I'm in character mode, I have to forget about good old Zach.

We can all relate to that, can't we? Before we go to work, family functions, social activities, etc., we often have to leave some of our burdens—stress, sadness, illness, self inflicted exhaustion, and so much more—behind. The show must go on, as they say, so embracing the M.A.S.K. helps ensure success when we're counted on the most.

Every Fan, Every Time

Early in my career as a mascot, I developed a mantra to live by no matter what kind of day I was having. It's quite simple: "Every fan, every time." It means that whenever my character would interact with someone, that person was going to get what they were looking for. Come hell or high water, I vowed to be consistently on my game, having a little mischievous fun and creating memorable experiences for everyone I met.

You can approach the people you meet in the same way. It might be a little more difficult without a fluffy suit on, but if you can bring your best to every encounter you have with a stranger—whether it's on a plane, in line at the bank, at a restaurant counter, or even in the stands at a ballgame—I can pretty much promise you that you'll have a better experience. And so will the other person.

Not everyone you meet in life is going to be nice (see chapter 5), but that doesn't mean that YOU can't be the one who's friendly and upbeat. I've been tired, over worked, and stressed out, but I try to put that all aside in an effort to engage and be present with everyone I meet.

I could think of a million excuses to avoid conversations, but what if I miss out on the game changer like I mentioned earlier? I firmly believe that you only get one chance to make a first impression, so I try to make the best one I can every single time—whether I'm in a costume or not.

A Harrowing Experience

The most dramatic example of this happened in 2010 when I was called to make an appearance at a high-rise office building in downtown Phoenix. All I knew was that I was going to entertain a group of Special Olympians and help them raise some money.

My mascot mask dictates that I be happy, entertaining, funny, adventurous, and a little cheeky. And that was definitely my intention when I showed up for the appearance. The person who met me told me that everyone was on the roof and that we'd be going up there right away. As we rode the elevator, I learned that they wanted me to rappel down the exterior of the building and that the local news was going to capture it all.

What no one knew was that Zachary Hall is terrified of heights. I always have been, and I always will be.

The idea of rappelling down a twenty-story building was really freaking me out, but my character wouldn't be afraid of heights. My character would enjoy rappelling down the building, making jokes along the way. And that's what everyone was expecting. How could some bozo named Zachary Hall screw this up?

Needless to say, I was having a serious internal dialog for the rest of the elevator ride. What it came down to was this: I could bow out and let everyone down, or I could accept the mission and do something legendary.

I decided to embrace my M.A.S.K., and I've been doing this stunt now ever since. I never enjoy it, but I've gotten more and more confident. The last time I went down, I took selfies with some of the office workers and played Rock-Paper-Scissors with someone on the fourteenth floor.

Every year my palms sweat and my heart beats faster, and I want to jump out of my skin when I'm standing at the top of the building. It takes a huge effort to lean backward and take that first step. I don't think I could EVER do it without my costume on, but with my costume on I get strength from the expectations of the people around me.

Can you relate to this moment? No matter what job you have, you've probably had days where you had to step out on a ledge and perform at a level you've never had to before. Now is the time to take this same approach as you build the best network possible.

Points Of Departure

- We all wear masks every day, we just don't often think about our roles that way.
- It's okay to be a little different within your mask. Masks give you superpowers!

Flight Pattern

How can you improve your Mindset, Attitude, Sense, and Knowledge to achieve more in your personal and professional life? Write ideas down for every mask you wear.

Build Your Network

Think about the people you meet, or would like to meet, while you're "in character." Write down the names, contact info (phone, email, twitter, etc.), and a short description of anyone who comes to mind. I'll get you started:

Name	Contact Info	Description
Eddie Matney	@EddieMatney	Celebrity chef
John Quinn	@JohnnyLasVegas	Hotel Executive
Ian Grushka	@PsychoSmoke	Bassist in the band New Found Glory

4 Follow Up– A Fantastic Force!

"A day or two after you meet someone, send them a handwritten letter."

So you're making all kinds of great contacts and building your network at a record pace—now what? It's time for the all-important follow up. In my view, follow up is the most important part of any connection.

I really can't stress this enough. Network connections aren't worth anything if they go stale, so I'm going to show you how to keep them fresh so they're always ready when you need them.

As soon as you meet someone, start preparing for following up. If you can, get the person's business card. It's the easiest way to get someone's physical address, phone number, email, job title, etc. It's filled with valuable information! The most important detail is the physical address, and I'll tell you why in a second. Having a business card also makes it easier to do online research on the person when you get home.

If you can't get a business card, try to get as much information as they'll give you and add it to your contacts: name (correctly spelled), address (most important thing), phone number, email address, etc.

And don't forget to add each new person to as many of your social media accounts as you can. Twitter is my go-to platform, but you should have all of them and be able to touch base with your connections on whatever networks THEY prefer.

When I met Dani Deahl the DJ on a flight to Detroit from Chicago, I knew she used Twitter to communicate. To this day I keep in touch with her, and learn more about her, through her tweets.

She's now an editor for *NYLON* and *DJ Mag*, so I get to hear about all the many DJs she supports. She even connected with a guy I went to high school with, and it's pretty cool that the three of us are now part of the same network. Thanks to social media, Dani and I have a much deeper relationship than we would have had if we had just exchanged business cards and left it at that.

Do Your First Follow Up The Old-Fashioned Way

A day or two after you meet someone—if you managed to get their business card or their mailing address in some other way—send them a handwritten letter. A real one. On paper. With a pen. You can always send an email or a text, but I've found that going old school with something tangible and real is the best way to go for that first touch point after your initial meeting.

Your note should do three things:

1. It should acknowledge your meeting and shared experience.

2. It should make you stand out and give them a reason to keep in touch with you.

3. It should plant the seed for a future meeting. I often suggest getting together for a coffee if we're in the same city, but you can recommend any other face-to-face way of keeping in touch that you like. If that's not in the cards, ask to connect on social platforms if you haven't already done so.

Working as a mascot made following up with people and hitting all three of these points pretty easy. I'd write my note on the team's letterhead and throw in my baseball card. It was a simple thing to do, but it made a HUGE impression.

I understand that you probably don't have official stationery or a baseball card with your picture on it, but that doesn't mean you can't get creative with your own approach. It doesn't even have to be over the top, but it should be genuine, showcase your uniqueness and indicate that you took some extra time to put it all together. If you sell Pepsi, like a friend of mine does, send your new connections a bottle or can of the stuff and remind them that you're the Pepsi guy.

Remember that couple I met in New York and the home-bottled wine they sent me? That was a great way to follow up! The possibilities are virtually limitless.

Just don't stress out over it. In today's world, even a simple handwritten note and a business card can make a big impression because very few people take the time to write notes anymore. Just be proud of who you are and what you do, and you'll go a long way toward deepening your connections.

Don't get upset if you send something awesome and don't get a response from someone. That happens all the time with bad bricks. Even good bricks may take a while to respond. It's not unusual for a few weeks to go by and out of the blue I'll get a call from a new connection, replying to my coffee invitation. This happens from time to time with government officials, business leaders, and other busy people, so be patient!

This is another reason why it's so important for you to enjoy your time with each new connection in the moment. Once the meal is over or the plane lands, life comes back full speed and responsibilities return.

Stay In Touch With Social Media

After that first flashy follow up, it's okay to rely on electronic forms of communication to stay connected over time. Social media makes it easier than ever—even our grandmas are on Facebook! And since social media platforms follow you wherever you go, they're much more stable over time than mailing addresses and email addresses.

As I mentioned, my favorite social media platform is Twitter. I tweet multiple times a day, pretty much every day. And I constantly check my feed to see what the people in my network are up to. If you're in my network and you tweet regularly, I'm likely to see you every day!

Social media is the best way to stay on people's minds with simple touch points. If you're not active on social media, you're missing many opportunities to strengthen and expand your network. There are different platforms for different relationships and comfort levels, so be cognizant of which platforms you're using and HOW you're utilizing them.

Keep Track Of Your Network As It Grows And Changes

As your network expands over time, people you've met will change jobs, move to new cities, start new ventures, get married, etc. With all these changes going on, following up will get more difficult and become more important than ever.

I suggest these two strategies to stay organized and up to date:

1. **Create email folders for all your connections.**

   I categorize these by year and how we met, such as on a plane, at a golf event, in a bar, or at a charity event.

2. **Create a database of all your connections.**

   This method continues to add value to my life. Having the name, company, title, phone, email, year met, how met, and maybe something special about everyone in my network all in one place is a great tool to have for myself or people I know who are traveling, looking for a job, or hoping to connect with someone with a certain expertise.

Points Of Departure

- Right after you meet someone new, send them a handwritten note.
- Use social media to keep up to date with everyone in your network. Even if you just like someone's post, your connection will feel the touch.
- As your network gets bigger, keep track of moves and changes with an Excel spreadsheet.

Flight Patterns

1. Make sure you're active on every major social media platform, and post something at least once a day, every day, for the next two weeks. By then it should become a habit!

2. Come up with some creative ways you can craft a memorable first follow up. Even if you just order some "great-to-meet-you" notes, you'll be way ahead of the game in a world where writing letters is a dying art.

3. Think of the people you haven't connected with in a while and make a point to reach out to them. Find out what they're up to and update their contact information, if applicable. Social media is fine, but you'll earn extra points if you meet with these people in person.

Build Your Network

Think of the people you catch up with on a regular basis and how important they are in your life. Don't you think you'll have just as great a relationship with more people if you take the time to follow up? Here are a couple people in my network who I'm in constant touch with:

Name	Contact Info	Description
Justin Roberts	@JustinRoberts	PA announcer/author
Dani Deahl	@DaniDeahl	DJ, Editor at large, DJ Mag
Kathy Nguyen	@Kathy.Nguyen.xo	Photo editor, The KNOT

5 Don't Be A Jerk

"When you try to make a connection and it goes badly, focus on the things you can control—your M.A.S.K.—and not on the things you can't, like how the other person reacts to you."

The world is filled with people you want to meet but who are going to let you down when you finally do make a connection. When someone like that bursts your bubble, it's going to hurt, but please don't let it deter you from building an awesome network. You can always grow from moments of disappointment, and you can always learn something about how NOT to act toward others when you come across a first-class idiot.

Every day, I think about the plethora of people who have accepted invitations to have coffee, breakfast, lunch or a drink with me; the people who have let me vent about my problems and then lifted me up; and the people who have provided me with a valuable contact or an opportunity to grow. I challenge myself and I challenge you, DON'T BE A CRUMBLY BRICK IN SOMEONE ELSE'S HOUSE!

I love the fact that I've committed to being a strong red brick for people, but I'm sure I've fallen short on more than one occasion. It happens to all of us. Sometimes we're caught off guard, or our minds are preoccupied with a specific concern or problem. All of that is excusable, but it's important to try to be open to people, especially as you get more successful.

Here are just a few examples of some people who let me down in my quest for the best network around. I share these stories only to illustrate the kind of person to avoid, and the kind of person you NEVER want to be.

I also want to remind you not to take bad behavior personally. When you try to make a connection and it goes badly, focus on the things you can control—your M.A.S.K.—and not on the things you can't, like how the other person reacts to you. They may even genuinely like you but still end up acting like an imbecile because they're distracted by a work crisis, worried about a medical issue, or just don't have enough time in the day. While some people are genuinely rude and obnoxious, try to cut everyone else—especially busy and successful people—a little bit of slack. Maybe the timing is off the first time you meet someone. They might come through for you the next time if you stay on the high ground.

The De-Mentor

During my final semester of college, I was in a leadership program that encouraged me to find a mentor, someone who could help me transition into the "real world" and push me toward my goals and dreams. The best part was that my mentor and I would share six biweekly dinners, paid for by the program.

At the time, I worked in the game-day entertainment department of the Phoenix Roadrunners, a minor league hockey team. I had identified someone in that organization who had an impressive entrepreneurial backstory as the perfect mentor for me.

I reached out to him and received a follow-up email from his assistant. I figured that would happen, and I knew I'd have to make this gatekeeper my ally. I called to introduce myself so she could put a voice to the email, and I sent a card to her office reminding her that I needed help securing my mentor.

Three months later, my leadership program ended and I was still without a mentor. While I missed all the free dinners, I was still interested in connecting with this man who I admired. I ran into him at an exhibition game and I hit him with an enthusiastic high five and a twenty-second elevator pitch about the whole mentor thing, hoping he'd put two and two together.

"I'm unfamiliar with you," he said. "Did you shoot me an email? Here's my email address. Send me one real quick and I'll get it on my phone."

Naturally, I pulled out my Palm Pilot (I was waaaaay ahead of my time as a nineteen-year-old), sent an email to the same address I'd been using, and sure enough—beep-beep-beep—his phone buzzed with my latest email.

Of course nothing transpired after that. Or the next time I saw him. Or the next. On the few occasions when I met him at various events around town, I would always look to STILL connect with him to learn about his story and his various interests.

Years later I even ended up sitting next to his wife at a basketball game and told her parts of this story. She got a kick out of it, and promised to give her husband my card after I told her how I'd been trying to get connected after all this time!

Nothing.

I used to get upset every time I reflected on this missed opportunity, but now I realize that I'm doing all right without this particular bad brick, or weed, depending on the analogy you prefer.

The Ungrateful Businessman

The kind of negative connection I hate the most is with a person who's mean to you even when you do something nice for them. Remember the laptop I found, which helped me bond with the watercolor lady?

Well, when I got off the plane I found the owner of that laptop in the airport. He was standing in front of the bathroom, frantically yelling at his traveling companion. I went up to him to save the day and make everything right in his world. "Excuse me, sir. Is this your laptop?" I asked.

The look on his face went from anger to surprise to embarrassment to gratitude in less than two seconds. "What can I do for you?" he asked. "How 'bout I just shake your hand!" He reached out his hand and I shook it. "Have a great day!"

That's literally all he said to me. That was the extent of his thank you. Not that I should have been expecting anything more, but come on. I pretty much saved his life! A decent person would have responded with a little more gratitude and humility, don't you think? What would you have done?

Half of me felt that he didn't deserve to get the laptop back. I wanted there to be a Yelp page about him where I could review his personality and warn anyone who's unlucky enough to do business with him. But then I realized it was more important for me to do the right thing and help someone than to expect something in return, even though it would have been the decent thing for him to do.

The Selfish Elected Official

I had a similar experience with a member of Congress from Arizona. I was in Washington, DC, and made an appointment to see this elected official because I'm interested in politics and just might like to lead a revolution some day. I arrived at the appointed time and introduced myself as Zach Hall.

Everything was going great until I got the question: "How's your dad doing?" This politician thought I was the son of a business leader who shares my last name, and when the realization hit that I wasn't related to this businessman, the meeting took a different tone and I was ushered out very quickly.

It was a completely humbling experience. Here I thought that I had a great opportunity to get some advice or direction from someone I looked up to, but it felt like it was really the politician who was looking for something.

I thought that maybe I just caught this person on a bad day, but just two weeks later we crossed paths in Arizona at a local fast-food chain of all places. I walked up to say hello and it was like we were meeting again for the first time. The politician didn't remember me until I gave him some hints. While I'm sure many of our local leaders meet thousands of people every month, it always boggles my mind that many of these leaders struggle with something as simple as connecting with their constituents.

This experience really taught me to never forget where I come from, or the fact that my behavior has the power to shape someone else's impression of me. This is just another reason why it's so important to embrace your M.A.S.K. at every possible moment. While I wasn't necessarily looking for anything in particular in each meeting, I look back on the way each interaction made me feel and that's the lesson I take here. DON'T BE A JERK.

Channel Your Inner Buddy

Just like Will Ferrell's character in the movie *Elf*, if you spread Christmas cheer in a world of cynics, or just bring a positive approach to each interaction, you always have the opportunity to be the most decent person in the room.

Whether you're waiting in a line, serving customers, or meeting a stranger on a plane, you can powerfully impact another person's life just by the way you interact with them.

As I travel through life—literally on planes and more figuratively through my daily journeys—I always do my best to maintain joyfulness and gratefulness like Buddy the Elf.

At a minimum, I always say "Hi" and "Thank you" to people. And most of the time I try to give the people I interact with at least one reason to think of me as a red brick, whether I have had my morning coffee or not. Even when I'm not feeling well, I work hard to put myself in the right mindset, which is the first and most essential element of embracing your M.A.S.K.

Points Of Departure

- Try to make a positive impression with every interaction. Even if you can't help someone the way they want you to help them, be nice and respectful.
- Move on from people who aren't willing to help you or who don't respond well to your own acts of kindness. The time you waste being sad or angry is better spent finding better people.
- Try to learn from the people who let you down. How could you have approached

them differently? Was something else going on in their lives that made them so inconsiderate? If nothing else, you'll get a clear example of how not to behave yourself.

Flight Pattern

Follow the Golden Rule in every interaction. If you're a consistently good person, you won't worry as much about the occasional jerk you run into.

Build Your Network

I'm not going to give you any names of the people who were jerks to me. Even though you might have better luck with them, I don't want to give them any free publicity! Instead, here are some connections that could have easily come off as jerks, but because they don't mince words and "tell it like it is," they've become some of my greatest contacts.

Name	Contact Info	Description
Steve Lueder	@SlippeOfficial	Music producer, entrepreneur
James Rhine	@JamesRhine	Big Brother contestant, actor, director of marketing
JD Whitfield	@TheActualJD	Radio Jock/DJ

6 You Can Never Know Too Many People

*"I love being the guy who knows the
right people. I love being able to refer
my friends to people who can help them.
It not only feels good, but it also gives
me credibility and acts as an insurance
policy for any future days when I need a
favor, advice, or something else."*

A bigger network means a bigger life. It's really that simple. The more people you can rely on in more places, the better your chances for helping yourself and others should the need arise.

It's not that you have to be super close with all your connections, or even that you'll ever call on all of them as the years progress, but it IS about being prepared for as many requests for help as possible.

These requests can be as mundane as restaurant recommendations or as life changing as smart career advice. Like I told you earlier, I can't WAIT for the day when someone asks me if I know anyone who teaches watercolor painting!

For me, the end game (if there even is one, and there really isn't) of networking is synergy. I love being the guy who knows the right people. I love being able to refer my friends to people who can help them. It not only feels good, but it also gives me credibility and acts as an insurance policy for any future days when I need a favor, advice, or something else.

What's more, as I meet new people and do new things professionally, everyone in my network wins through my own growth and development. For instance, a great friend of mine owns one of the coolest taco shops in Scottsdale, Arizona, a place called Diego Pops. It's always the first place I think of when I'm planning to meet new people for lunch, happy hour, or dinner. So not only do I win by building new relationships when I meet people there, but my friend also wins when I expose his business to new customers.

I'm passionate about people, and the only competition I want to be in with the rest of humanity is the one that decides who can help the most. My quest for connections is a lifelong pursuit that evolves and grows every single day.

Once you start networking, you'll never want to stop!

But, Zach, Doesn't Networking Just Happen On Its Own?

Sure it does! As social creatures, we meet people and grow our networks all the time. We do it naturally. Organically.

My point is that networking becomes exponentially more powerful when we do it with INTENTION. All the benefits, including the potential for positive change, get magnified. Why wouldn't we want that for ourselves and the other people in our lives?

If you're content to limit yourself, or to just rely on whatever connections happen randomly in your life, that's fine. But I suspect that if you're reading this far along in this book, you might want to go out and make as many great connections as possible.

Make "NETWORK, NETWORK, NETWORK!" your rallying cry. Live by the old saying that "It's not WHAT you know, it's WHO you know." And as long as we're talking about old sayings, you can use this one, too: "The more the merrier!"

When you're building a network with intention, you really can't know too many people. I've met several small business owners and CEOs in my life and, as an entrepreneur, I want to keep meeting people like this. I want to have as many people to contact at all times so I have a better chance of getting the advice and guidance I need to succeed. I might even be able to get a job if I need one!

What's really cool is that most successful businesspeople love talking to enthusiastic, ambitious people with dreams of their own success. My raw energy and eagerness to learn has, on more than one occasion, given powerful CEOs a jolt of passion that's reinvigorated their own careers. You might find some business bigwigs who think they're too good for you, but you really don't want to talk to those kind of people anyway.

I always tell people that I've never given my business card to anyone who didn't need it. I create opportunities to connect because I know that I can be of service to the people in my network. New people I meet might not see it that way, or it may take them a while to come around, but that's not going to stop me from putting myself out there.

It's Easier To Meet People When You Know Who You Are

I'm always telling people that they have to work on their personal brands. If you just thought to yourself that the word "brand" could be another word for "mask," give yourself a gold star!

In whatever role you're playing, you really have to know who you are and how to communicate that to others. If you're a Pepsi salesman, be the Pepsi guy. If you're a singer or a painter, be confident about your craft in every situation. Lead with your passion and your brand will come shining through.

You can have more than one brand—the social you, the employee you, the artist you, the entrepreneurial you, etc.—but don't get too carried away, and be sure you're focused and consistent about which mask you're wearing when.

Make Sure You've Got A "Guy" For That

Of all the masks I wear, one of my favorites is being the guy with all the "guys." When you think of your own network, who is that person for you? Who do you call when you need a plumber, a wedding photographer, or a career coach? You can post your requests to everyone on Facebook, but who is the person, or who are the people, who always seem to come through for you?

I LOVE being able to find people for my friends, family members, and other connections. If you need one, I've got a taco guy for you. Or a car wash guy. Or a writer guy. Even a watercolor lady! This is really the main reason to have a network in the first place—to live a service-driven life through connections that can help yourself and other people.

I identify everyone in my network by the masks they wear, by what kind of "guy" or "gal" they are. This makes everyone a lot easier to remember, and a lot easier to refer.

Learn How To Get Help

Not everyone is good at accepting help, but if you think about it, people helping people makes the world go round. Even the strongest, most productive among us can't do everything alone. That's why we need to make connections. That's why we need "guys" and "gals" to help us when we can't do something for ourselves or for someone we want to help out.

Not having much as a kid probably made me more reliant on connections than most people. I knew from an early age that the only way I could get ahead was with the help of others. But I've found that no matter how successful I get, I'm still going to need help getting to the next level, and the next, and the next. This is the difference between a handout and a hand up. When you're given a handout it can feel like charity, but when you're given a hand up you get an opportunity to shine or grow. I'm grateful for the help I receive, and I use every hand up I get to create synergy within my network. And I try as much as possible to be the person who gives others a hand up when they need one. It's a chance for me to see others reach their fullest potential and become stronger parts of my own network. It's a definite win-win!

Connections can get you into restaurants without reservations and into careers in the sports industry. They can get you into wild parties in Las Vegas. They can save you money or ensure that you don't get ripped off. They can enrich your lives in ways you can't even imagine—they can even help you write and publish a book!

It's great to be self-reliant—and you'll have to be when it comes to growing your network and working your connections in the beginning—but it's also important to be open to the help, advice, and assistance your network can provide.

When you were young, your family members were most likely your main source of support and advice. As a young adult, you added friends and, if you were really lucky, mentors to the list. And now your professional network is on the way to becoming another important asset as you continue your life's journey.

Get A Great Connection In Vegas

Vegas is a town where almost everybody is either in, or has a connection to, the hospitality industry. And if you don't have an insider who can make sure you have a great time, you haven't really been to Vegas.

A few years ago I met Pearce Cleveland, the marketing director of a popular day club on the Las Vegas Strip. He was taking care of my group of friends, which happened to include two professional athletes. Naturally, we were seated at a reserved private cabana and given the royal treatment. I quickly identified Pearce as the "guy."

Being realistic with myself, I knew that my next trip to Vegas without any pro athletes wouldn't be anything like the experience I had that day. But I found every opportunity to talk with Pearce, mostly about being a mascot and my approach to networking. We quickly connected because he felt as strongly as I do about the importance of good people helping each other out.

A few months later, I took care of a big client of Pearce's at my work, which made Pearce look like a superstar. While it's good to never keep score when doing favors for others, he was adamant about owing me one the next time I was in Vegas! So during Thanksgiving break in 2014, I decided to take my dad on the trip of a lifetime. We had both done Vegas on our own many times, but never together. I contacted Pearce, and he took charge.

When my dad and I walked into one of the top Vegas hot spots, we saw a projected sign that read "Light Nightclub Welcomes Zach & Randy Hall." We were seated at a private table featuring my dad's favorite cigarettes and beverages. It just went on and on, and a simple trip became a lifelong memory thanks to the right connection. No money exchanged hands—the experience was built on the foundation of two people leveraging each other's abilities for mutual benefit.

Being A "Guy" or "Gal" Makes You More Important

I met my friend Jeffrey Nguyen in a leadership workshop. One day he invited me out for coffee to talk about becoming more engaged with people. As an assembly line manager for Pepsi, his biggest concern was how to manage people who were older than he was. "How can I get them to believe in me?" he asked.

Just like I told you to look for clues about people when you meet them on a plane, at a bar, or anywhere else, I told Jeffrey that the best way to connect with people is to know something special about them. If they like football, for example, ask them how their team did every week. Empathy and understanding go a long way toward building respect and loyalty.

After that meeting, we decided to grab lunch on another occasion to talk about how Jeffrey could expand his presence in the community and get better at networking. When we met at the restaurant, he gave me a big case of Gatorade. "You just made an impression on me," I told him. "I'll never forget that you're the Gatorade guy!"

He told me that his company was actually owned by Pepsi, so he really became the Pepsi guy. And you know something? Dr. Pepper is my favorite soda, but I drink more Pepsi nowadays because I have a Pepsi guy!

We all have something to share, and becoming that "guy" is a great approach to marketing yourself and getting people to be part of your "brand." When you're someone's "guy" or "gal," you've built a relationship that's much more powerful than any kind of commercial advertisement.

Not All Tacos Are Created Equal

As I mentioned earlier, my friend Cory owns a cool taco shop in one of the most popular tourist areas in the country. I love going to Diego Pops, not just because of the people watching and the good food, but also because it's my "guy's" place. He's the taco guy!

In my mind, Cory's tacos are better than anyone else's! We call him Diego and he embraces it, which makes it even more enjoyable to go there whenever I can and recommend it to just about everyone I meet. If you're ever in Scottsdale, tell them that Zach sent you!

Over the years Cory has run a variety of restaurants in the Phoenix market, including Majerle's sports bars. Cory has become a successful restaurateur by honoring the time-tested hospitality mantra of building at least six regulars every day. Talk about the fact that you can never know too many people!

While many restaurants can offer much of the same stuff on a menu, it takes a special person to make connections that keep people coming back for more. Take this same approach in your own career, or in the things you're most passionate about. Create regulars in your life who become your fans. How cool is that?

You can serve up a better taco, or anything else for that matter, by sharing your energy, your dreams, and your goals with everyone you encounter.

Points Of Departure

- When it comes to networking, more is ALWAYS better.
- The only thing you should be competing with other people for is the title of who can help the most people.
- Once you start networking with intention, you'll never want to stop.
- It's great to have "guys" and "gals" you can call on for help.
- Being a "guy" or "gal" carries with it a certain level of importance.
- Brand yourself as a specific kind of "guy" or "gal" to make a bigger impression on everyone you meet.

Flight Patterns

1. Meet as many people as you can on a given day, or in a given week or month. Set a benchmark and then try to beat it on a regular basis.

2. What kind of "guy" or "gal" are you? Make a decision and think of cool ways you can burn that idea into the heads of everyone you meet. After you figure yourself out, go through your network and decide what kind of "guy" or "gal" all your connections are. If you're really ambitious, you'll organize all your contacts like I do!

Build Your Network

Think of all the "guys" and "gals" you know. Here are a few of mine:

Name	Contact Info	Description
Pearce Cleveland	@SirPearce	Nightlife and hospitality professional
Jeffrey Nguyen	@thejeffreynguyen	Pepsi guy
Cory Adams	@coryadamsbrah	Taco guy—Diego Pops, Scottsdale, AZ

7 Let's Grow Our Networks Together

"My contacts are all waiting to hear from you. In return, I hope you'll share some of the people you know with me. If we can grow our networks together, we'll both be unstoppable!"

All networking, personal and professional, should be targeted. To meet the kinds of people you want to meet you have to be strategic about where you sit on a plane, the bars and restaurants you frequent, the events you attend, the colleagues you connect with, etc.

As your network grows with the right people, those same people advance your strategic targeting by introducing you to people they know, and it just multiplies from there.

Let me give you a weird example of how this works: In Phoenix, we have the greatest networking event in America, a fun and hugely popular professional golf tournament. Corporate boxes that go for tens of thousands of dollars line the fairways, and companies of all sizes clamor to get one so they can entertain clients all week long.

Each year more than 300,000 people, including myself, flock to this event to enjoy the beautiful weather, the people watching, the occasional golf shot, and the natural connecting that takes place among the fun-loving attendees.

I was twenty-four years old when I went to my first Phoenix Open, and I vowed that I'd never miss this event going forward. And as my network has grown over the years, so has my ability to get into some of the swankier corporate functions. During my first visit in 2011, I had a one-day, Corporate Village pass for the 18th hole. It was cool, but it wasn't the party I saw taking place on holes 16 or 17.

By 2016, I had access to my pick of corporate boxes and parties. I was in networking heaven, and I rubbed elbows with a wide variety of CEOs, pro athletes, celebrities, and more. Friends and strangers alike kept introducing me to new people with different backgrounds, occupations, and beverage preferences. No one cared where anyone was from—what mattered most was that we were all there together having a good time.

The Spirit Of Sharing

When I think about growing networks, I think about my friend Tyler. You already know him—he's the guy I took with me to the all-star football game, and the couples we were with gave us money to build a football field for the Boys & Girls Clubs.

Tyler is a real hustler in the best sense of the word. After he spent a few years working for the Boys & Girls Clubs, he took a job at a local business that specializes in food and beverage marketing and community events. One of the first things he did was ask me to look at my contacts because he wanted to find new people he could do business with.

Seeing someone's passion lights me up, so of course I gave Tyler my spreadsheet of more than 600 names, and he ran with it. He emailed a variety of my contacts individually. He introduced himself and made funny comments about me to break the ice.

One person he reached out to was no longer with the company I knew him from, but that didn't stop Tyler. He ended up meeting the guy who replaced the person I knew and turned that meeting into more than $100,000 in new business.

We're In This Together

Nothing makes me prouder than being the catalyst for people like Tyler, who used just one of my contacts to generate $100,000 in mutually beneficial business.

Another example of sharing my contacts to help people succeed involves my friend Mike Spangenburg, co-founder of the lifestyle brand State Forty Eight Clothing. This guy is passionate about the state of Arizona and has some of the coolest local gear around. As his T-shirts and tank tops continue to sell, his network continues to grow.

After I met Mike for the first time, I helped him start a marketing fire. As a fellow Arizona native, I became a fan of the brand that Mike and his partners had created. I wanted to get in touch so I followed their company on Instagram and asked to connect. After that I shared a variety of contacts, from World Series hero Luis Gonzalez to a friend of mine from lululemon, who have helped State Forty Eight achieve tremendous growth.

My passion truly is people, and that includes you. It's why I wrote this book. And it's why I included the names and contact information of some of my best contacts at the end of each chapter. I encourage you to reach out to them— they're all waiting to hear from you!

You can find even more of my contacts at DontSleepOnPlanes.com. In return, I hope you'll share some of the people you know with me. If we can grow our networks together, we'll both be unstoppable!

Are You A Spark Plug Or A Butt Plug?

I will ALWAYS remember what my first boss—Tom Wyse from the Rollero Family Skating Center in Maryvale, Arizona—said to me when I was ten years old: "Zach, you can be a spark plug or a butt plug. One stinks and the other drives the world. Which one do you want to be?"

Ever since I heard those attention-getting words, I've tried to be the best spark plug I could possibly be. I hope I sparked YOUR interest in effective networking, and I hope you'll decide to be a spark plug for others, too.

All the tools you need are in this book, and all I ask is that you give it time and celebrate your connections as you continue to create and deepen them. There are many tremendous people in this world, and some of them are literally just a quick "hello" away from making a difference in your life. Try not to focus on the almighty dollar when you meet people. This can be difficult if you're young and impatient and want more out of your career, but I'm here to tell you that networking is about more than increasing your net worth. Sometimes just a good conversation is a success, whether it leads to a future opportunity or not. Over time, when you look at your network as a whole, I guarantee that all the effort you put into it will make your life a bit more fun, happy, and successful in lots of different ways.

So keep meeting people, handing out business cards, embracing your M.A.S.K., following up, sharing meals, conversing on planes, staying in touch, connecting people, asking for advice, doing acts of kindness, sharing your contacts, and asking for and accepting help when you need it. You're sure to rack up many "cosmic victories" that will come back days, months, or even years later to enrich your life in surprising ways.

You have nothing to lose and everything to gain, so get out there and be the spark plug that drives the world around you.

Points Of Departure

- To meet the people you want to meet be strategic about where you sit on a plane, the bars and restaurants you frequent, the events you attend, the colleagues you connect with, etc.
- Don't be afraid to share your connections and be a catalyst for other people's success. It's a great feeling!
- Be the spark plug that drives the world around you!

Flight Patterns

1. Contact at least five of the connections I've given you in this book (or at DontSleepOnPlanes.com) and see what happens. If you make a connection,

please let me know about it at
Zach@DontSleepOnPlanes.com
2. Share your connections with friends and
   ask them to share theirs. Grow your networks together!

Build Your Network

Think about the people you've met because
someone introduced you. Here are a few great
connections I've made through referrals:

Name	Contact Info	Description
Mike Spangenberg	@StateFortyEight	Co-founder, State Forty Eight Clothing
StrawberryRadio	@StrawberryRadio	Radio DJ
Scott Lazerson	@ScottLazerson	Connector

Acknowledgements

So many people helped me turn the idea for this book into the reality you're now holding. I owe a debt of gratitude to everyone who's helped shape my life, including bosses, friends, neighbors, servers, family members, and strangers.

To Dad: Thanks for allowing me to learn from my mistakes, and from the reasons I chose to make those mistakes in the first place. I become more like you every day, and I'm thankful for that as well.

To Mom: Thanks for always supporting my crazy ideas. I love that I have your spirit of adventure and drive for fun!

To Meryl: I love you so much and am grateful that you're by my side. Thank you for being my soul mate and supporting me as I reach for my dreams. I look forward to adventuring together side by side 'til death do us part.

To Ashton, Codey, & Danielle: Thanks for encouraging me as big brother to be the fun and outgoing one at all our family events. I love you guys and can't wait for all our adventures to come.

To Ed: Thank you for believing in this book and helping to bring it to life. I hope it is the first of many.

To Carol: Thanks for making sure I dotted all the i's and crossed all the t's.

To Tom & Beth Wyse: Thank you for mentoring me, and for teaching me to connect with people through the random jobs you gave me. I'm a spark plug because of you!

To Kevin Treacy: Thank you for taking an 18 year old Great Skate assistant manager, eager to lead a business I grew up in, and shaping me into a community minded, Christ centered business leader.

To my ridiculously random network: Thanks for sharing your time and insights with me. Your genuine conversations and encouragement made this book possible.

To my future seatmates: Get ready for the conversation of a lifetime.

About The Author

Zachary Hall has spent the majority of his career performing for millions of people as a sports entertainment professional. He's managed roller skating rinks, thrilled arena

@ZacharyHall
@ZacharyHall

audiences dunking basketballs, donned various professional mascots, emceed corporate team builders, and even learned to make balloon animals while walking on stilts in college.

Over the years, Zach has built an impressive social network that includes professional athletes, entertainers, entrepreneurs, artists, business leaders, and government officials.

He loves meeting new people, and sees every random human encounter as an opportunity to make a life-changing connection.

Zach@DontSleepOnPlanes.com

Made in the USA
San Bernardino, CA
06 September 2017